Capstone Curriculum Publishing

Photo-Illustrated Biographies

Capstone Curriculum Publishing materials are published by Capstone Press
P.O. Box 669, 151 Good Counsel Drive, Mankato, Minnesota 56002

http://www.capstone-press.com

ISBN 0-7368-7115-2

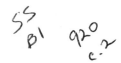

Photo-Illustrated Biographies

Table of Contents

Photo-Illustrated Biographies

Skills Correlation Chart

Book Title	Reading Strategies	Graphic Organizers	Study Skills
Susan B. Anthony	Sequence of Events	Using a Cause-and-Effect Chart	Using a Thesaurus
Alexander Graham Bell	Making Inferences	Using a 5 W's Chart	Using an Encyclopedia
George Washington Carver	Main Idea and Supporting Details	Using a Main Idea Chart	Using an Encyclopedia
Cesar Chavez	Fact and Opinion	Using a K-W-L Chart	Using an Almanac
Frederick Douglass	Summarizing	Using a Sense Chart	Using the Parts of a Book
Amelia Earhart	Comparison and Contrast	Using a Venn Diagram	Using the Internet
Thomas Edison	Making Inferences	Using a 5 W's Chart	Using an Encyclopedia
Chief Joseph	Fact and Opinion	Using a K-W-L Chart	Using an Almanac
Florence Nightingale	Comparison and Contrast	Using a Venn Diagram	Using the Internet
Eleanor Roosevelt	Summarizing	Using a 5 W's Chart	Using a Dictionary
Elizabeth Cady Stanton	Making Inferences	Using a Sense Chart	Using the Parts of a Book
Sojourner Truth	Cause-and-Effect	Using a Cause-and-Effect Chart	Using a Dictionary
Harriet Tubman	Cause-and-Effect	Using a Cause-and-Effect Chart	Using a Dictionary
Booker T. Washington	Main Idea and Supporting Details	Using a Main Idea Chart	Using an Encyclopedia

Introduction to *Photo-Illustrated Biographies*

Photo-Illustrated Biographies is a series of 4-color books designed to help at-level and reluctant readers enjoy true-life stories of great leaders and innovators from American history. The series has a strong multicultural focus, and lively texts describe both the struggles and lasting impact of people such as Susan B. Anthony, Booker T. Washington, Amelia Earhart, Cesar Chavez, and Eleanor Roosevelt. These high-interest, nonfiction books are written for readers at Grade 2–3 levels, but should interest students through Grade 5.

Purposes ■ This guide and the student **Activity Sheets** included in it will:

- Strengthen students' understanding of reading strategies, graphic organizers, and study skills that will help them read nonfiction.
- Prepare students to take standardized tests.
- Expand students' experience with science and social studies content.

Classroom Management ■ This guide's general framework provides you with a flexible tool for efficient classroom management, regardless of how you make the reading assignments. It is designed for use with any or all of the books in the *Biography* series. You may wish to assign the same book to several students or different books to each student. A specific title can also be assigned for independent, paired, small cooperative-group, or whole-class reading.

Home-School Connection ■ Suggest to the class that they talk with their families about favorite role-models from history. Then have students interview an older family member to create a Personal Biography. Tell them to use any tools available, including tape recorders and videos, and then ask the person they are interviewing about:

- Childhood memories: When, where, and how did you grow up? Tell me about your family.
- Your own personal heroes from American history or from the country of your birth: How have they inspired you and affected your life?

Strategic Reading

Reading is a process that requires an active relationship between the reader and the text. Before, during, and after reading, good readers use specific techniques and strategies to compare their background knowledge and previous experience with what they are reading. This guide suggests methods and strategies you can use to help students succeed in understanding nonfiction.

Student Activities ■ In support of this goal, this guide contains four kinds of Activity Sheets—Comprehension, Reading Strategies, Graphic Organizers, and Study Skills. The **Skills Correlation Chart** on page 1 suggests which Activity Sheets to use for each book. In addition, charts on pages 5, 6, and 7 provide specific teaching suggestions for effective use of the Activity Sheets.

Exploring Prior Knowledge/ Building Background Knowledge

Encouraging students to share prior knowledge and experience can benefit those who need additional background. Questions such as the following can serve as discussion prompts:

- Do you have family in other countries? See if you can find out about relatives you don't know. Maybe you can get their addresses and start a correspondence by letter or e-mail.
- What are the most important dates in your own life so far? Ask your parents about the most important dates in their lives. Include births, marriages, careers, important moves, achievements.

Vocabulary

Building a strong vocabulary is a key factor in developing a positive attitude toward reading. The books in this series have been written to help students understand and master unfamiliar vocabulary. At the back of each book, a **Words to Know** section contains definitions and phonetic respellings of key words. In the text itself, words are defined in context at point of use and specialized words are followed by phonetic respellings.

Capstone • *Photo-Illustrated Biographies Teacher's Resource Book*

Words to Know ■ You may want to use this section to preteach the vocabulary before students read the book. You might have students:

- Create personal dictionaries in their notebooks or journals by recording words and definitions that were difficult for them.
- Use the words in oral or written sentences.
- Redefine unfamiliar vocabulary in their own words.

Setting a Purpose for Reading

Some students may wish to know more about other people mentioned in their book. Some students might want to know more about the work the person they read about performed. Help students set a purpose for reading, by guiding them to:

- Identify the title of the book.
- Scan the book, looking at the headings, illustrations, captions, and features (such as the **Table of Contents, Words to Know, Useful Addresses, Internet Sites** and **Index**.
- Begin a K-W-L Chart to identify what the students already know about a topic and build on this knowledge to ask new questions. This chart can be done as a small-group or whole-class activity. Create the chart on the board or provide students with Graphic Organizer 6: Using a K-W-L Chart. Have students complete the first two columns. During or after reading, have students complete the third column.

K - W - L CHART		
K	**W**	**L**
Many famous people in history were born poor.	What traits of character helped them become leaders or creators?	
Both men and women have had to fight for their rights and freedom.	Which rights and freedoms are important to me in America?	

Suggestions for Reading

Here are some reading methods you may wish to use to customize instruction to your students' strengths:

Reading Methods

 Independent Reading

Have students analyze short sections of the book at a time. Have them write questions that arise from their reading and relate these questions to what they already know. If the answers to their questions are easily accessible and vital to their understanding, have students find answers before continuing to read. Otherwise students can compile their questions for each section and research the answers after reading.

Using the Activity Sheets

As students read, have them complete a Reading Strategy Activity Sheet to monitor their own reading. See the **Skills Correlation Chart** on page 1 for suggestions on which strategies to use for each selection.

 Paired Reading

Have partners take turns reading aloud pages or chapters. Suggest that they tell each other in their own words the main points of what they have read. Students can synthesize their ideas and come up with a summary.

 Small-Group Reading

Arrange students in cooperative groups to read the books, one chapter at a time. Assign specific responsibilities to individual group members to foster cooperative learning. For example, one student can be the recorder and take notes, while another serves as facilitator to keep the discussion on task. Another can record the questions and another can summarize the answers.

 Whole-Class Reading

The *Biography* series can be used to supplement various curriculum areas. For example, if you are teaching a geography unit about the different states, you may wish to circulate one or more of these books for reading and discussion about a leader's contribution.

Meeting Individual Needs

Implementing instructional strategies that meet the needs of individual students creates a learning environment that maximizes students' potential for success. Suggestions for use before, during, and after reading follow:

Limited-English Proficiency

Second-Language Learners will benefit by partnering with an English-proficient reader who can read the text aloud while the second-language learner follows along. Point out the text's visual and graphic elements to facilitate understanding of key ideas and concepts. For example, encourage second-language learners to look through the photographs and identify the leader, an important person in the leader's life, and an action by the leader that made a difference.

Learning Styles

Auditory Learners rely principally on what they hear to process information. To maximize their success, pair auditory learners and have them take turns reading the book aloud to one another. Keep the readings relatively brief, and have these students present frequent oral summaries to each other.

Kinesthetic Learners are adept at processing information through bodily sensations. Provide them with opportunities to use body language to demonstrate what they have read. For example, students can:

- Work in groups to stage a mock rally or strike. Have them make signs and banners. Invite groups to perform their project in front of the class and have students guess which leader was involved.

Visual Learners process information best when they see it. Have them examine the photographs in each book.

- Students might use photographs of leaders when they were young to document their own lives. They could bring in family snapshots and write or talk about someone who is important in their life.

Integrating Activity Sheets with the Reading

The primary purpose of reading nonfiction is to acquire information. This guide features four types of Activity Sheets to help students with this goal. The Activity Sheets are designed to give reluctant and at-level readers practical and concrete ways to help them organize and assimilate information. The chart below shows the purpose of each type of Activity Sheet.

ACTIVITY SHEET	PURPOSE
Comprehension	To assess overall comprehension, including vocabulary, literal recall, inferential thinking, and students' ability to respond to open-ended questions.
Reading Strategies	To help students identify particular techniques used by nonfiction writers to organize and express ideas.
	To teach students to use their identification of specific techniques as an aid to reading comprehension.
	To help students relate their own experiences to the reading in order to make meaningful connections.
Graphic Organizers	To provide students with concrete frameworks that enable them to use strategic approaches to help their reading comprehension.
Study Skills	To help students understand information-gathering techniques to be used in writing a research paper.

The Comprehension Activity Sheets are book-specific. The other Activity Sheets are generic in nature but have been carefully correlated so that they can be applied to one or more titles in the series. The **Skills Correlation Chart** on page 1 suggests which Activity Sheets to use with specific books.

Capstone • *Photo-Illustrated Biographies Teacher's Resource Book*

....

Teacher's Resource Book • Photo-Illustrated Biographies / 5

Reading Strategies
Activity Sheets

The following chart suggests how to use and teach
Reading Strategies Activity Sheets.

READING STRATEGIES	TEACHING SUGGESTIONS
Cause and Effect	Causes can have multiple effects. For example, ask students to list some of the effects of Thomas Edison's inventions. Eleanor Roosevelt worked hard all her life caring for other people. One effect—as First Lady she received about 30,000 letters a month from people asking for her help with problems— caused another effect: Later she was named U.S. delegate to the United Nations to work for world peace and human rights.
Comparison and Contrast	Comparing and contrasting helps students identify unstated similarities and differences. For example: Chief Joseph was a Native American and Frederick Douglass was an African American. Both were citizens of the United States who worked for freedom and equal rights for all Americans.
Making Inferences	Strategic readers make inferences when they use information in the text to make reasoned assumptions about a point the writer is making indirectly. Point out that valid inferences are based on details, facts, and examples.
Fact and Opinion	Point out to students the difference between a fact and an opinion. Examples: Cesar Chavez started a union called the United Farm Workers in 1962. (*fact*) Today, farm workers are happy with their working conditions. (*opinion*) In addition, guide students in evaluating the source of information before they decide if the information is factual.
Main Idea and Supporting Details	The main idea is the key point of a reading. This may be directly stated or can be inferred from information in the paragraph. A main idea is usually supported in the paragraph by facts and details.
Sequence of Events	Information can be organized by understanding the order in which events occur. Clue words such as *first, next, later, then,* and *last* signal the order of events.
Summarizing	Information can be organized by readers restating what has been learned in their own words. A good summary is brief and includes only the important information. A summary need not be done for a whole book; it can be done at the end of a chapter or a section.

Graphic Organizers
Activity Sheets

Graphic organizers are conceptual frames to aid students in organizing information as they read. Organizers also can be used to generate thoughts for writing. These suggestions can be used with the organizers in this guide.

GRAPHIC ORGANIZERS	TEACHING SUGGESTIONS
Using a Cause-and-Effect Chart	There are many variations in cause-and-effect relationships. A graphic organizer can help readers identify specific causes and effects in a text.
Using a K-W-L Chart	A K-W-L Chart can be used before, during, and after reading to set and check purposes for reading.
Using a Main Idea Chart	Recording each main idea and its supporting details is a good way to remember what a book is about. Identifying main ideas and details can also help in summarizing.
Using a Sense Chart	Categorizing information according to the five senses helps readers absorb meaning.
Using a Venn Diagram	A Venn Diagram highlights similarities and differences between two or more things. Similarities should be recorded in the overlapping section, and differences in the individual sections.
Using a 5 W's Chart	Good readers can often summarize, generalize, or draw conclusions by asking themselves questions that begin with a *w*: who, what, when, where, why.

Capstone • *Photo-Illustrated Biographies Teacher's Resource Book*

Study Skills Activity Sheets

These Activity Sheets are designed to help students develop the skills they will need to complete research assignments. Use the following teaching suggestions to introduce each sheet.

STUDY SKILLS	TEACHING SUGGESTIONS
Using an Almanac	The table of contents and index of an almanac can be used to find important, up-to-date information about well-known people. For practice, ask students to look in the index for such topics as *Presidents of the U.S., Scientists, Sports Personalities,* or *Noted Personalities,* and then find a specific person who interests them.
Using an Encyclopedia	Encyclopedia articles often have subheads, maps, and illustrations that can help students locate and understand information. Cross-references can also lead students to additional information on a topic. You might pick a topic linked to the person the students read about. For example, if they read about Harriet Tubman, ask them to look up *Slavery, Abolition,* or *Underground Railroad.*
Using the Internet	The Internet is a marvelous source of information that is constantly changing. Help students to understand that researching on the Internet is different from looking information up in an encyclopedia. Explain that information provided by the government or a university (addresses ending in .gov or .edu) is usually more reliable than information provided by organizations (addresses ending in .org) and by commercial advertisers (addresses ending in .com). **Note:** Because of constant updating, some Internet addresses provided in the student books may no longer be in use. The Internet addresses provided on the activity sheets are the most current available. It is recommended that the teacher check the site before the lesson.
Using the Parts of a Book	The Table of Contents and Index can help students locate specific information. Some books also have features such as sidenotes and footnotes, a list of maps and graphs, and a handbook of special terms and definitions. Using another text, model how its different parts can be used to find information.
Using a Thesaurus	A thesaurus can help students to enrich their vocabulary as they find synonyms and antonyms for a specific word.

Connecting Reading and Writing

Writing an Informational Article

When students have finished reading about a particular leader, they can write an informational article of their own. Encourage them to choose a part of the biography requiring some further research. Remind them of how they used their Reading Strategies Activity Sheets and tell them that they will follow the same techniques when organizing their own article.

I. Prewriting

Students can use prewriting techniques such as brainstorming and freewriting to find and develop their topic.

Choosing a Topic ■ Ask students to brainstorm a list of ideas from the book that they would like to research further. You might suggest the following examples:

- A grown-up who played an important part in the person's life.
- The importance of confidence in becoming a leader.
- How poverty or hardship affected the person.

Limiting the Topic ■ Once students have selected a topic, suggest they narrow it so that they can write about it in one or two pages. For example, if students choose to write about the importance of confidence in becoming a leader, they may want to focus on the childhood, teenage, and adult experience of one important figure, such as Eleanor Roosevelt.

Using the Study Skills Activity Sheets ■ After students have selected and narrowed their topic, make the Study Skills Activity Sheets available. Explain that they can use these Activity Sheets to help locate the information they need. For example, students can use Study Skill Activity Sheet 1: Using an Encyclopedia to understand how the information in an encyclopedia is organized. This will help them find the facts they need. Students can use Study Skill Activity Sheet 3: Using the Internet to locate useful Web sites, and Study Skill Activity Sheet 4: Using an Almanac to find up-to-date statistics. Students can use Study Skill Activity Sheet 5: Using a Thesaurus to help them make varied and interesting word choices.

II. Drafting

After students have gathered and organized their ideas, it is time to begin writing. Be sure students understand that a draft is a work in progress. Encourage them not to worry about spelling, grammar, usage, and mechanics at this point. They will deal with these during the revising and proofreading stages.

Using the Graphic Organizers Activity Sheets ■ The Graphic Organizers Activity Sheets can help students prepare their research papers. Help students select the graphic organizer that best suits their needs. If the student has narrowed a topic to The Great Depression, you might suggest that he or she use Graphic Organizer Activity Sheet 3: Using a 5 W's Chart— who, what, where, when, and why— to help organize research information and outline the report. Another useful Activity Sheet might be Graphic Organizer 1: Using a Main Idea Chart to help students outline information before they write.

III. Revising

After students complete a rough draft of their work, they should revise it. Students should focus on the overall organization of their paper, making sure that information is accurate, clear, and logical. Remind students that they can add or delete information as necessary. Next, students should focus on improving the paper's grammar, mechanics, and word choices. As a final part of the revision stage, students may exchange papers with a classmate for peer evaluation. The focus of peer review at this stage should be on overall content—accuracy, completeness, and coherence. Encourage students to identify strengths first in their peers' writing, and then areas that need improvement.

Capstone • *Photo-Illustrated Biographies Teacher's Resource Book*

Using the Reading Strategies Activity

Sheets ■ If students chose to model their paper after a specific Reading Strategy Activity Sheet, they should check their revised draft against that to make sure they followed the structure accurately. For example, if students used the Cause-and-Effect Activity Sheet, they should check to see that the paragraphs in their report, and their report as a whole, make cause-and-effect relationships clear.

IV. Proofreading

At this stage, students should read their papers carefully in order to correct mistakes in grammar, punctuation, and spelling. They should pay particular attention to subject-verb agreement, pronoun-antecedent agreement, spelling and capitalization of proper names, and correct use and spelling of homonyms (such as *their*, *there*, and *they're).* Peer review is also helpful at this stage.

V. Publishing

Students can "publish" their work in book form, selecting which information goes on each page. Those who are comfortable with word processors might choose to input their articles and print them out. Encourage students to embellish their work with drawings, captions, graphs, charts, and so forth. Cooperative groups might produce an anthology.

WRITING TOPICS SUGGESTIONS

Cesar Chavez and His Fight for Justice

Susan B. Anthony, Activist for Women's Rights

Chief Joseph, a Wise Leader of the Nez Percé

George Washington Carver, Creative Scientist

How Eleanor Roosevelt Worked for Human Rights

The Mystery of Amelia Earhart and the Disappearing Airplane

Metacognition

Understanding how their own thinking process works can help some students become better readers. After students have completed their writing assignments, have them discuss how their reading helped them in their writing. Suggest that students ask themselves questions such as: What was the hardest part of the writing process for me? How did the information I read help me get past this difficulty? Here are some example problems and solutions:

- *I couldn't think of a topic.*
  The student might look back at the book and review the chapter heads.

- *I didn't know where to begin writing.*
  The student might review how the author began the book or look at models of expository writing.

- *I couldn't decide what was important to include.*
  The student might review the kinds and numbers of details the author included.

Encourage students to use self-evaluation and analysis as tools in all of their school work. Discuss with them how the entire experience of connecting their reading with their writing can help them in other curriculum areas.

An answer key for the Comprehension Activity Sheets is provided on page 10. You may use this key to check students' responses, or you may choose to copy and distribute the answers for students to check their own work.

Answers are not provided for the Reading Strategies, Graphic Organizers, and Study Skills Activity Sheets. These are designed to encourage a variety of responses as students exercise critical thinking. Students might work in small groups or with a partner to exchange papers, compare answers, and share opinions as a peer-review and self-evaluation experience.

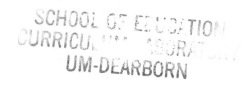

Answer Key

Biography:
Susan B. Anthony
Comprehension 1

A. 1. suffrage
2. convention
3. petition
4. articles

B. 5. A own property
6. B many people
7. A voting
8. B dollar coin

C. *Possible response:* The 15th Amendment gave African American men the right to vote. But it did not give women the right.

Possible response: They were both interested in women's rights. Elizabeth gave speeches and wrote articles. Susan set up meetings. When Elizabeth was home with her children, Susan could travel and speak.

Biography:
Alexander Graham Bell
Comprehension 2

A. 1. invention
2. probe
3. communicate
4. read lips

B. 5. A his brother died of tuberculosis
6 C deaf
7. B his son died from breathing trouble
8. A started Bell Telephone Company

C. *Possible response:* He and his brother built a speaking machine out of tin and rubber. They shaped it like a human head. The noise was so real that it fooled the neighbors. They thought it was a real baby. Then he experimented with his dog. He noticed that growling was similar to talking.

Possible response: He invented the telephone. This allowed people to talk from very far away. They did not have to wait days or weeks for mail to arrive. News could travel instantly. Families could communicate more easily and more often than before.

Biography: George
Washington Carver
Comprehension 3

A 1. experiment
2. tutor
3. botany
4. kidnapped

B. 5. B was an African American
6. B Tuskegee Institute
7. A grow healthy crops
8. C protect peanut sales in the U.S.

C. *Possible response:* George really liked to write letters and many people wrote him. Then his name was just George Carver. There was another George Carver, and their mail got mixed up. So, Carver added a "W" to his name to avoid confusion. It didn't stand for anything, but people thought it stood for "Washington." They started to call him that.

Responses will vary. Accept all reasonable responses.

Biography:
Cesar Chavez
Comprehension 4

A. 1. union
2. public
3. strike
4. slave

B. 5. A fight
6. B vote
7. A Chavez was dead
8. C support

C. *Possible response:* They can make sure that farm workers get treated fairly. They can support the workers if they go on strike for better pay and conditions.

Possible response: A fast showed that Cesar was strong. He went for many days without food. People paid attention to him.

Biography:
Frederick Douglass
Comprehension 5

A. 1. slave catchers
2. abolitionist
3. mush
4. plantation

B. 5. B He taught himself.
6. A He was too much trouble.
7. A a newspaper
8. C He was not safe in the United States.

C. *Possible response:* Once slaves could read they would be able to find out all sorts of information. They would be able to educate themselves. Educated people would be more difficult to keep in slavery.

Possible response: Frederick Douglass fought for the rights of all people. His actions helped end slavery and get the right to vote for women.

Capstone • *Photo-Illustrated Biographies Teacher's Resource Book*

Biography: Amelia Earhart Comprehension 6

A. 1. A beliefs
2. B navigator
3. A equator
4. C social worker

B. 5. C pilot
6. D passenger
7. B women's rights
8. E disappeared

C. *Possible response:* She saw wounded soldiers returning from World War I and she wanted to help them, so she became a nurse's aid. The patients who were pilots told her their stories. She was very interested in their stories.

Possible response: Earhart's grandmother did not punish the sisters for freeing the horse. Instead, the grandmother scolded the horse's owner. Earhart learned that the reasons you do something are as important as what you do. She learned that it was important to do something if she thought it was right.

Biography: Thomas Edison Comprehension 7

A. 1. C patent
2. D record
3. B laboratory
4. A assistants

B. 5. A and taught him on the farm
6. A slept in his laboratory
7. B tap words on his knee in Morse Code

C. *Possible response:* He invented a talking doll by putting a small phonograph inside a doll. He could record a human voice. He also invented the light bulb. He made the world's first movie camera. These helped him earn the nickname "wizard" because these inventions seemed like magic tricks, and a wizard can make magic.

Possible response: Edison's inventions made future inventions possible. For example, the phonograph led to tape recorders and CD players. The moving picture led to movies, videos, and television.

Biography: Chief Joseph Comprehension 8

A. 1. surrendered
2. treaty
3. reservation
4. homeland

B. 5. C gold
6. A move
7. A hot swamp
8. B fight no more

C. *Possible response:* The Nez Percé did not all go back to their homeland in Idaho. Chief Joseph was sent to a reservation in Washington. This made him very sad.

Responses will vary. Accept all reasonable responses.

Biography: Florence Nightingale Comprehension 9

A. 1. C profession
2. D sanitary
3. A advice
4. E wealthy

B. 5. respected
6. God's will
7. infections
8. British Red Cross

C. *Possible response:* She made people aware of how unclean hospitals really were. She started a school. She taught her students how to help the doctors instead of just being maids.

Possible response: She stayed in bed but kept working. She helped make British government hospitals more sanitary. She also wrote a report that led to better health care in India.

Biography: Eleanor Roosevelt Comprehension 10

A. 1. B volunteers
2. A First Lady
3. C confidence
4. B Depression

B. 5. rights
6. uncle
7. walk
8. radio

C. *Possible response:* She visited army hospitals all over the world. She was the First Lady. She raised their spirits.

Possible response: She went to places where he could not go. She gave speeches. She talked to the people.

Biography:
Elizabeth Cady Stanton
Comprehension 11

A. 1. C movement
2. B legislature
3. A Abolitionists
4. B Amendment

B. 5. rights
6. convention
7. Susan B. Anthony
8. children

C. *Possible response:* Judge Cady knew that women didn't have many rights. They could not own property or sue people in court. They could not vote. They could not attend most colleges. Men could do all of these things.

Possible response: She said that women should have the same rights as men. She said that women should be able to vote. She said that many women agreed with her, and asked her to speak.

Biography:
Sojourner Truth
Comprehension 12

A. 1. equality
2. lawyer
3. slave-trader
4. dishonest

B. 5. A a farmer bought her freedom
6. B he was afraid of his owner
7. C their children would be slaves

C. *Possible response:* She talked about God, slavery, and women's rights. God was the most important to her. She left New York City because she wanted to travel and tell people about her love for God. She said that God was her only master and that he was truth. Her faith gave her courage to give speeches.

Possible response: She wanted to let people know that just because she was a woman it didn't mean she wasn't strong and able to do things. She showed everyone her strong arms and told about the hardships of slavery. She showed that women could be very strong.

Biography:
Harriet Tubman
Comprehension 13

A. 1. C conductor
2. E freed
3. D earn
4. A bloodhounds

B. 5. to safe houses
6. led slaves farther north to Canada
7. women
8. poor and older African Americans

C. *Possible response:* She went into enemy territory to spy on troops. She even went on a rescue mission to free slaves. Tubman served in the army for three years.

Possible response: She was one of 11 children. Her name was Minty until she was 13, then her family changed it to Harriet. She worked in her owner's house as soon as she was 6 years old. She cleaned the house and took care of a baby. Harriet Tubman's owner was cruel to her. She was hungry and had no soft place to sleep. She tried to escape once but she got tired and went back.

I am most amazed that as a young girl she was brave enough to refuse to help her owner capture a runaway slave.

Biography:
Booker T. Washington
Comprehension 14

A. 1. D spokesperson
2. C educator
3. B plantation
4. A agriculture

B. 5. go to school
6. they were freed
7. hard work
8. three times

C. *Possible responses:* Washington felt that education should lead to a job. He felt that students should learn to think and write poetry, and learn job skills.

Responses will vary. Accept all reasonable responses.

Activity Sheets

Graphic Organizers

Study Skills

Teachers using *Photo-Illustrated Biographies Teacher's Resource Book* may reproduce Student Activity Sheets in complete pages in quantities for classroom use.

Biography: *Susan B. Anthony*

Name _____ Date _____

A. Choose the word below that best completes the sentence. Write the word on the line.

articles	convention	legislature	petition	suffrage

1. Susan B. Anthony fought for woman _____, the right to vote.

2. A group of women met at a _____ to discuss their rights.

3. Susan got about 400,000 people to sign a _____.

4. In her newspaper, Susan printed _____ about equal rights.

....

B. Fill in the circle in front of the correct choice.

5. Susan thought it was not fair that women could not _____.

   Ⓐ own property   Ⓑ be teachers   Ⓒ have jobs

6. Susan's petition showed legislators that _____ wanted women's rights.

   Ⓐ only women   Ⓑ many people   Ⓒ she and Elizabeth

7. Susan broke the law by _____.

   Ⓐ voting   Ⓑ suffering   Ⓒ giving a speech

8. The U.S. government put Susan's picture on a _____.

   Ⓐ dollar bill   Ⓑ dollar coin   Ⓒ book

....

C. Pick one of the questions below. On the back of this sheet, write a brief paragraph to answer it.

- Why do you think Susan B. Anthony might have been disappointed by the 15th Amendment?
- Why were Susan B. Anthony and Elizabeth Cady Stanton such an effective team?

Biography: *Alexander Graham Bell*

Name _____ Date _____

A. Choose the word or words that best complete the sentence. Write the answer on the line. There are more words than sentences.

communicate	invention	listen	probe	read lips

1. Alexander Graham Bell's most famous _____ was the telephone.

2. A _____ could help find metal in patients who had been shot.

3. When people _____, they share ideas.

4. Bell taught deaf students how to_____.

B. Fill in the letter of the response that best completes the sentence.

5. Bell's family moved to Canada after _____.

   (A) his brother died of tuberculosis   (B) the Civil War broke out   (C) a famine started

6. Bell had a special interest in helping _____ people.

   (A) poor   (B) blind   (C) deaf

7. After _____, Bell invented a special jacket to help people breathe.

   (A) his wife got asthma   (B) his son died from breathing trouble   (C) President Garfield was shot

8. Bell _____ since so many people wanted to own telephones.

   (A) started Bell Telephone Company   (B) asked the government for money   (C) gave phones away for free

C. Pick one of the questions below. On the back of this sheet, write a brief paragraph to answer it.

- Describe some of Bell's early experiments.
- How did Bell change the world forever?

Name _____ Date _____

A. Choose the word that completes the sentence. Write the word on the line. There are more words than sentences.

botany	experiment	kidnapped	tutor	slave

1. George Washington Carver liked to _____with plants.

2. Carver's owners hired a _____to teach him about science.

3. Carver decided to study _____ so that he could learn more about plants.

4. When Carver was a boy, he and his mother were_____.

....

B. Fill in the letter of the response that best completes the sentence.

5. Carver was turned away from two different schools because he _____.

   Ⓐ had poor grades   Ⓑ was an African   Ⓒ had no money
                              American

6. Carver spent most of his life teaching at _____.

   Ⓐ Highland College   Ⓑ Tuskegee Institute   Ⓒ Diamond Grove

7. Carver taught farmers how to _____.

   Ⓐ grow healthy crops   Ⓑ grow tobacco   Ⓒ pick peanuts

8. In 1921, Carver asked Congress to pass a law to _____.

   Ⓐ free slaves   Ⓑ give money to   Ⓒ protect peanut
                         his school   sales in the U.S.

....

C. Pick one of the questions below. On the back of this sheet, write a brief paragraph to answer it.

- How did George Washington Carver get the "Washington" in his name?
- Carver was a caring teacher. Describe a caring teacher you have known. What made that teacher special?

Name _____ Date _____

A. Choose the word below that best completes the sentence. Write the word on the line.

boycott	public	slave	strike	union

1. Cesar Chavez started a_____ of farm workers.

2. The march gained the attention of the _____.

3. The grape pickers stopped working and went on_____.

4. Chavez's father was treated like a _____ on a Mexican farm.

....

B. Fill in the circle in front of the correct choice.

5. Cesar Chavez would not _____ because he was against violence.

   Ⓐ fight   Ⓑ pick grapes   Ⓒ use pesticides

6. Chavez helped people sign up to _____.

   Ⓐ own a farm   Ⓑ vote   Ⓒ march

7. Chavez's wife accepted the Presidential Medal of Freedom because ____.

   Ⓐ Chavez was dead   Ⓑ Chavez was shy   Ⓒ it was for her

8. To _____ Chavez, truck drivers stopped carrying grapes.

   Ⓐ boycott   Ⓑ beat   Ⓒ support

....

C. Pick one of the questions below. On the back of this sheet, write a brief paragraph to answer it.

• How can people continue the work that Chavez began?

• Was fasting a good way for Chavez to get people to listen to him? Why or why not?

Name _____ Date _____

A. Choose the word or phrase that completes the sentence. Write your answer on the line.

1. After Frederick Douglass escaped, he had to hide from_____.
    (A) abolitionists   (B) slave catchers   (C) freedom fighters

2. A(n) _____writes and speaks out against slavery.
    (A) marshal   (B) slave owner   (C) abolitionist

3. As a child, Douglass was given_____ as his only meal.
    (A) mush   (B) stew   (C) steak

4. Douglass worked in the fields at a_____.
    (A) factory   (B) plantation   (C) small farm

B. Fill in the letter of the response that best answers the question.

5. How did Douglass learn to read?
    (A) He paid a private tutor . (B) He taught himself. (C) He went to school.

6. Why was Douglass sent to Baltimore the second time?
    (A) He was too   (B) The Civil War began.   (C) His mother died.
    much trouble.

7. What did Douglass create that helped slaves communicate?
    (A) a newspaper   (B) underground tunnels   (C) a radio

8. Why did Douglass go to England?
    (A) He wanted   (B) His grandparents   (C) He was not safe in
    to visit.   lived there.   the United States.

C. Pick one of the questions below. On the back of this sheet, write a brief paragraph to answer it.

- Why do you think Mr. Auld thought slaves should not learn to read?
- What are some things Douglass did to make the United States a better country?

Name _____ Date _____

A. Choose the word or phrase that best completes the sentence. Write the answer on the line.

1. Amelia Earhart's parents taught her to stand up for her _____.

   Ⓐ beliefs   Ⓑ money   Ⓒ horse

2. A_____ reads maps and helps the pilot get to the right place.

   Ⓐ passenger   Ⓑ navigator   Ⓒ writer

3. Earhart wanted to fly around the earth near the _____.

   Ⓐ equator   Ⓑ date line   Ⓒ Pacific Ocean

4. In Boston, Earhart was a _____who helped children.

   Ⓐ reporter   Ⓑ nurse   Ⓒ social worker

B. Fill in the letter of the answer that best completes the sentence.

A. doctor	B. women's rights	C. pilot	D. passenger	E. disappeared

5. After Earhart visited Canada, she went to school to become a _____.   Ⓐ Ⓑ Ⓒ Ⓓ Ⓔ

6. On Earhart's first flight across the Atlantic, she was a _____.   Ⓐ Ⓑ Ⓒ Ⓓ Ⓔ

7. Earhart and Eleanor Roosevelt gave speeches in favor of _____.   Ⓐ Ⓑ Ⓒ Ⓓ Ⓔ

8. On Earhart's final flight, she and her navigator _____.   Ⓐ Ⓑ Ⓒ Ⓓ Ⓔ

C. Pick one of the questions below. On the back of this sheet, write a brief paragraph about it.

- How did Amelia Earhart's visit to her sister in Canada help her to later become a pilot?

- What do you think the story about the milkman's horse taught Earhart?

Capstone • *Photo-Illustrated Biographies Teacher's Resource Book*

Name _____ Date _____

A. Choose the word that best completes the sentence. Fill in the circle that matches the letter of the word.

| A. assistants | B. laboratory | C. patent | D. record | E. telegraph |

1. An official paper that protects an invention is called a _____.

   Ⓐ   Ⓑ   Ⓒ   Ⓓ   Ⓔ

2. People were amazed that Thomas Edison could _____ a human voice.

   Ⓐ   Ⓑ   Ⓒ   Ⓓ   Ⓔ

3. As a child, Edison experimented in a _____ in his basement

   Ⓐ   Ⓑ   Ⓒ   Ⓓ   Ⓔ

4. Edison had many _____ to help him with his experiments.

   Ⓐ   Ⓑ   Ⓒ   Ⓓ   Ⓔ

B. Write the letter of the correct answer on the line.

5. Edison's mother took him out of school _____.

   Ⓐ and taught him on the farm   Ⓑ so he could work at home   Ⓒ and sent him away to boarding school

6. Edison was so dedicated to his work that he sometimes_____.

   Ⓐ slept in his laboratory   Ⓑ dreamed about it   Ⓒ forgot to eat

7. After Edison became almost deaf, his wife would_____.

   Ⓐ ask his friends to use sign language   Ⓑ tap words on his knee in Morse Code   Ⓒ shout very loudly

C. Pick one of the questions below. On the back of this sheet, write a brief paragraph to answer it.

- What are some of the amazing inventions that earned Thomas Edison the nickname "The Wizard of Menlo Park"?
- What do people mean when they say that Thomas Edison invented the future?

Name _____ Date _____

A. Choose the word below that best completes the sentence. Write the word on the line.

| homeland | reservation | settled | surrendered | treaty |

1. After three months of fighting, Chief Joseph _____.

2. The Nez Percé signed a _____ with the U.S. government.

3. The U.S. government set aside land in Idaho for a _____.

4. Chief Joseph wanted the Nez Percé to keep their _____.

B. Fill in the circle in front of the correct choice.

5. Many white settlers came to Nez Percé land to find _____ .

Ⓐ shells Ⓑ edible roots Ⓒ gold

6. The U.S. Army ordered the Nez Percé to _____ .

Ⓐ move Ⓑ give up their horses Ⓒ go to Canada

7. Many Nez Percé died in Kansas because their new home was a _____ .

Ⓐ hot swamp Ⓑ snowy mountain Ⓒ cold canyon

8. In Chief Joseph's famous speech, he said that he would _____.

Ⓐ camp in Montana Ⓑ fight no more Ⓒ see the president

C. Pick one of the questions below. On the back of this sheet, write a brief paragraph to answer it.

- Why do you think his doctor said that Chief Joseph died of a broken heart?

- If you were Chief Joseph, would you have joined the chiefs who wanted war? Why or why not?

Capstone • Photo-Illustrated Biographies Teacher's Resource Book

Name _____ Date _____

A. Choose the word below in the box that best matches the definition. There are more words than definitions. Fill in the circle that matches the letter of the word.

A. advice	B. clean	C. profession	D. sanitary	E. wealthy

1. a job that requires special training   (A) (B) (C) (D) (E)

2. free from germs   (A) (B) (C) (D) (E)

3. ideas about how to make something better   (A) (B) (C) (D) (E)

4. having a lot of money   (A) (B) (C) (D) (E)

B. Choose the best answer for each question. Write the correct answer on the line.

5. Florence Nightingale showed that nurses should be _____.
   paid   sent to war   respected

6. Nightingale believed it was _____ that she become a nurse.
   practical   God's will   her parent's dream

7. During the Crimean War, more soldiers died from _____ than from battle wounds.
   poor diet   head injuries   infections

8. Florence Nightingale helped start the_____in 1870.
   British Red Cross   American Red Cross   Crimean Nurses
                                                          Association

C. Pick one of the questions below. On the back of this sheet, write a brief paragraph about it.

- How did Florence Nightingale change the nursing profession?
- How did Florence Nightingale respond to her illness?

Capstone • *Photo-Illustrated Biographies Teacher's Resource Book*

Name _____ Date _____

A. Fill in the circle in front of the word that best completes the sentence.

1. Eleanor Roosevelt led _____, people who work without pay.

Ⓐ delegations   Ⓑ volunteers   Ⓒ women

2. Eleanor was married to the president, so she was the _____.

Ⓐ First Lady   Ⓑ Governor   Ⓒ Red Cross

3. At school, Eleanor began to have _____ and believe in herself.

Ⓐ polio   Ⓑ memorial   Ⓒ confidence

4. Thousands of people lost their jobs in the Great _____.

Ⓐ Deal   Ⓑ Depression   Ⓒ Declaration

B. Read each question. Look at the possible answers in the box. There are more answer choices than questions. Choose the best answer for each question. Write it on the line.

cousin	hear	radio	rights	television	uncle	walk

5. People will be treated fairly if they have human_____.

6. Eleanor's_____ was president when she got married.

7. Eleanor helped her husband because he could not _____.

8. Eleanor used the _____ to tell people how she and the president would help the country.

C. Pick one of the questions below. On the back of this sheet, write a brief paragraph to answer it.

• Why do you think soldiers loved Eleanor during World War II?

• How do you think Eleanor helped her husband become president?

Capstone • *Photo-Illustrated Biographies Teacher's Resource Book*

Name _____ Date _____

A. Fill in the circle in front of the word that best completes the sentence.

1. Elizabeth Cady Stanton started a _____ for women's rights.

   (A) suffrage   (B) college   (C) movement

2. New York's _____ did not make the laws fair for women.

   (A) lawyers   (B) legislature   (C) judges

3. _____ like Elizabeth's husband were against slavery.

   (A) Abolitionists   (B) Conventions   (C) Congressmen

4. The 19th _____ gave women the right to vote.

   (A) Commandment   (B) Amendment   (C) Department

B. Read each question. Choose the best answer from the choices in the box. There are more answer choices than questions. Write the answer on the line.

children	Congress	convention	rights	Susan B. Anthony

5. Judge Cady could not help women because they had few_____.

6. Elizabeth and Lucretia Mott planned a _____in New York.

7. Elizabeth wrote speeches for _____.

8. Elizabeth could not always travel because she had_____.

C. Pick one of the questions below. On the back of this sheet, write a brief paragraph to answer it.

- Why do you think Elizabeth's father wanted her to be a son? Explain.
- What do you think Elizabeth said when she spoke to the New York legislature?

Name _____ Date _____

A. Choose the word in the box that best completes each sentence. There are more words than definitions. Write the word on the line.

equality	sojourn	lawyer	dishonest	slave-trader

1. Sojourner Truth wanted _____ for all people so they would be treated the same.

2. A _____ spoke for Truth in court and helped her get her son back.

3. A _____ bought and sold Truth's brothers and sisters.

4. The leaders in Truth's church were _____ and blamed her for another leader's death.

....

B. Fill in the letter of the phrase that best completes the sentence.

5. Sojourner Truth became free after _____.

   Ⓐ a farmer bought   Ⓑ she escaped   Ⓒ New York passed
      her freedom   to Michigan   a law to free slaves

6. Truth's son said he didn't know her in court because _____.

   Ⓐ he had forgotten   Ⓑ he was afraid   Ⓒ he wanted to live
      his mother   of his owner   with someone else

7. Slave owners wanted slaves to marry so that _____.

   Ⓐ they would   Ⓑ they could   Ⓒ their children
      be happy   live together   would be slaves

....

C. Pick one of the questions below. On the back of this sheet, write a brief paragraph to answer it.

- Of the three things Truth talked about when she gave speeches, which do you think was the most important to her? Explain.

- What was the main point of Truth's "Ain't I A Woman" speech?

Name _____ Date _____

A. Choose the word in the box that best completes the sentence. Fill in the circle that matches the letter of the word.

| A. bloodhounds | B. Civil War | C. conductor | D. earn | E. freed |

1. Harriet Tubman was a _____ on the Underground Railroad. Ⓐ Ⓑ Ⓒ Ⓓ Ⓔ

2. The Emancipation Proclamation _____ all slaves in the south. Ⓐ Ⓑ Ⓒ Ⓓ Ⓔ

3. When you work for pay, you _____ the money. Ⓐ Ⓑ Ⓒ Ⓓ Ⓔ

4. Dogs that find people by smell are called _____. Ⓐ Ⓑ Ⓒ Ⓓ Ⓔ

B. Circle the word or phrase that best comples the sentence.

5. Tubman helped slaves escape by getting them _____.

   clothing   transportation   to safe houses

6. When people offered a reward for her capture, Tubman _____.

   stopped helping   was caught   led slaves farther
   slaves   north to Canada

7. After slavery ended, Tubman helped _____ earn the right to vote.

   blacks   women   slaves

8. The Harriet Tubman home was a place for _____.

   poor and older   blind people   orphans
   African Americans

C. Pick one of the questions below. On the back of this sheet, write a brief paragraph to answer it.

   • Why do you think people called Harriet Tubman, General Tubman?
   • Describe Harriet Tubman's childhood. What amazes you most about her and why?

Biography: *Booker T. Washington*

Name _____ Date _____

A. Choose the word that best matches the definition. Fill in the circle matching the letter of the word. There are more words than definitions.

| A. agriculture B. plantation C. educator D. spokesperson E. honorary |

1. someone who speaks for others   Ⓐ Ⓑ Ⓒ Ⓓ Ⓔ
2. one who teaches and helps run schools   Ⓐ Ⓑ Ⓒ Ⓓ Ⓔ
3. a large farm   Ⓐ Ⓑ Ⓒ Ⓓ Ⓔ
4. the science of farming   Ⓐ Ⓑ Ⓒ Ⓓ Ⓔ

B. Circle the word or phrase that best completes the sentence.

5. Booker T. Washington wanted to _____ instead of working in the salt mines.

   teach school   go to school   work as a janitor

6. Washington and his family moved to West Virginia after _____.

   they were freed   his father bought a farm   they escaped the South

7. Washington wanted African Americans to prove they should be treated equally through_____.

   protests   hard work   debates

8. Washington was married_____ .

   once   two times   three times

C. Pick one of the questions below. On the back of this sheet, write a brief paragraph about it.

- Booker T. Washington said that farming was as important as poetry. Explain what he meant by that.
- Would you have liked to be a student at Tuskegee Institute? Why or why not?

Capstone • *Photo-Illustrated Biographies Teacher's Resource Book*

Name _____ Date _____

Main Idea and Supporting Details

> The **main idea** is the most important idea in a section. Other sentences in the section give **supporting details**. Supporting details tell more about the main idea. The main idea may be stated in a single sentence. Sometimes the main idea is not stated. Then readers must look for clues to decide what the main idea is.

A. Reread page 7. Then answer these questions.

1. What is this section about? _____

_____

2. What is the main idea of this section? _____

_____

3. What are three important supporting details in this section?

_____

_____

B. Reread the last paragraph on page 9.
Is the main idea of the paragraph stated in a sentence? _____

If yes, write the sentence on the lines below. If no, write your own main idea sentence.

_____

_____

C. On the back of this sheet, write a paragraph that tells something you learned about the person in this book. Make sure you include a main idea sentence and some supporting details.

Reread your paragraph. Underline the main idea sentence of your paragraph. Circle the supporting details.

Name _____ Date _____

Cause and Effect

> A **cause** is why something happens. An **effect** is what happens. Sometimes clue words such as **because** can help you recognize cause and effect.

A. Use your book to answer these questions.

1. Cause and effect can help you understand why something happened. For example, Abraham Lincoln died **because** John Wilkes Booth shot him.

    Cause: John Wilkes Booth shot Lincoln.
    Effect: Lincoln died.

    What is something that happened to the person in your book?

    EFFECT:_____

    Why did this happen?

    CAUSE: _____

2. Cause and effect can help you understand why someone did something. For example, Harriet Tubman helped hundreds of slaves to escape on the Underground Railroad. She wanted to stop slavery.

    Cause: Harriet Tubman wanted to stop slavery.
    Effect: She helped slaves to escape on the Underground Railroad.

    In the book you just read, what important thing did someone do?

    EFFECT:_____

    Why did the person do this?

    CAUSE: _____

....

B. Reread page 19. Find an example of cause and effect. Write your example on the lines.

    EFFECT: _____

    CAUSE: _____

Capstone • *Photo-Illustrated Biographies Teacher's Resource Book*

Name _____ Date _____

Making Inferences

> Writers do not always tell readers what they think or know. Sometimes the reader must use information from the text to **make an inference**. Then the reader must decide what the writer means.

A. Write your answers on the lines. Use the book to help you.

How does the writer feel about the person in your book? What information helped you to make this inference?

INFERENCE: _____

_____

_____

INFORMATION: _____

_____

_____

How do you think other people felt about this person? What information helped you to make this inference?

INFERENCE: _____

_____

_____

INFORMATION: _____

_____

B. Sometimes you can make an inference based on another person's behavior. For example, if a person is crying, you might infer that he or she is unhappy. On the back of this sheet, list three things the person you read about did. For each thing, make an inference about why he or she did it.

Name _____ Date _____

Summarizing

> **Summarizing** helps readers to recognize the most important ideas in what they read. When you summarize a nonfiction topic, you use your own words to tell the **main idea** and give some **supporting details**.

A.   Reread page 11. Write your answers on the lines.

1.   What is the title of the section?_____

_____

2.   Add your own words to make the title into a complete sentence.

_____

_____

3.   Does your sentence tell the main idea of the section?_____

If not, write a main idea sentence for the section._____

_____

_____

4.   What are the main events in this section? Retell these events in your own words.

_____

_____

_____

_____

B.   You just summarized page 11. Now reread page 13. Summarize it on the back of this sheet. First make a main idea sentence. Then add sentences with supporting details.

Biography

Name _____ Date _____

Comparison and Contrast

> A **comparison** tells how things are similar or alike. A **contrast** tells how they are different.

A. Read the section about the person's childhood. Then read one section about the person's life as an adult. Now answer these questions.

1. How was the person's life as a child similar to the person's life as an adult?

   SIMILAR: _____

   _____

   _____

2. How was the person's childhood different from his or her adulthood?

   DIFFERENT: _____

   _____

   _____

B. Compare and contrast two people you have read about. Write their names below. Make a list of how they are similar and how they are different.

Name 1: _____

Name 2: _____

SIMILAR	DIFFERENT

Name _____ Date _____

Fact and Opinion

> A **fact** is a statement that can be proved to be true. An **opinion** is a statement of what someone thinks or believes.

A.   Answer the questions below. Use the book to help you.

Reread page 15. What are three facts you learned? Write them below.

Fact 1: _____

Fact 2: _____

Fact 3: _____

What opinions did people have about the person you are reading about? Find two opinions anywhere in the book. Write them below.

Opinion 1: _____

_____

Opinion 2: _____

_____

B.   Write your answer on the lines below.

What was your opinion of this person before you read the book?

My opinion before reading: _____

What facts in the book changed or supported your opinion?

Facts: _____

_____

What is your opinion of this person after reading the book?

My opinion after reading: _____

_____

Capstone • *Photo-Illustrated Biographies Teacher's Resource Book*

Name _____ Date _____

Sequence of Events

Sequence is the order in which things happen. Paying attention to the sequence of events will help you understand what you read.

A. Answer the questions below. Write your answers on the lines. Use the book to help you.

Reread page 21. List three things that happened to the person you read about. Write them in the order they occurred.

FIRST _____

NEXT _____

LAST _____

B. List three important things that the person you read about did. Write them in the order they occurred. Use the book to help you.

FIRST _____

_____

SECOND _____

_____

THIRD _____

_____

Reread the three events above. Did the person you read about make life better or worse for other Americans? Why?

_____

_____

Name _____ Date _____

Using a Main Idea Chart

> A **Main Idea Chart** can help you to focus on the most important idea in a paragraph or section. Then you can use this chart to find the **supporting details**. When you write, you can organize your ideas in a Main Idea Chart. This can help you decide which details are important to include.

A. Think about the life of the person you just read about. What do you think was the most important thing that person did? Reread the section of the book that tells about that action. Write the main idea of the section in the top box of the Main Idea Chart. Next, write supporting details in the other boxes. You do not need to fill in every box.

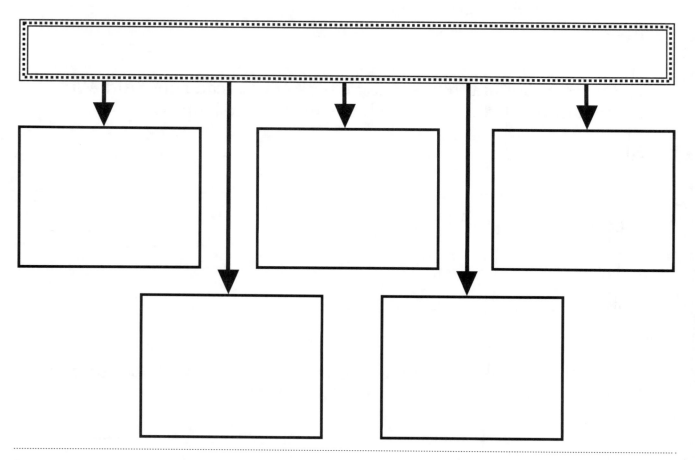

B. Choose another section of the book you just read. Then copy the Main Idea Chart onto the back of this sheet. Fill in the chart. List the main idea of the section and any details you find.

Name _____ Date _____

Using a Cause-and-Effect Chart

A **cause** is why something happens. An **effect** is what happens. When you read, use a **Cause-and-Effect Chart** to keep track of events and their causes. When you write, use a Cause-and-Effect Chart to organize information.

How does the book you read explain the main events and actions in this person's life? Use the Cause-and-Effect Chart for your answer.

In the book, find an important event or action in the person's life. Write it in the Effect box. Then, find out what made it happen. Write it in the Cause box at left.

Find more important events and their causes, and complete the chart.

CAUSE: Why Something Happens	EFFECT: What Happens

Name _____ Date _____

Using a 5 W's Chart

> Asking the questions **who**, **what**, **where**, **when**, and **why** can help you understand what you read. It can also help you when you write.

A. Choose one of the topics below from the book you have read. You can also suggest a topic of your own.

- The Person's Childhood
- How the Person Changed the World
- The Person's Professional Life
- **My Topic Idea** _____

Choose one of the topics above to write about.

MY TOPIC: _____

Look through your book to find information about the topic you chose. Use the 5 W's Chart below to help you organize your information. Answer as many of the 5 W's as you can. You may not be able to find an answer for each of the 5 W's.

Who?
What?
Where?
When?
Why?

B. Use the back of this sheet to answer the question below.

A 5 W's Chart can help you take notes to write a report. How might the chart be helpful?

Capstone • *Photo-Illustrated Biographies Teacher's Resource Book*

Name _____ Date _____

Using a Sense Chart

> We get information from the world around us through the use of our senses. We **see**, **hear**, **feel**, **smell**, **touch** and **taste**. Use a **Sense Chart** to help you when you read.

A. On the top line, write the name of the person you read about.

Name _____

In the chart, write in each triangle how the person you read about used that sense.

You do not have to write in every triangle.

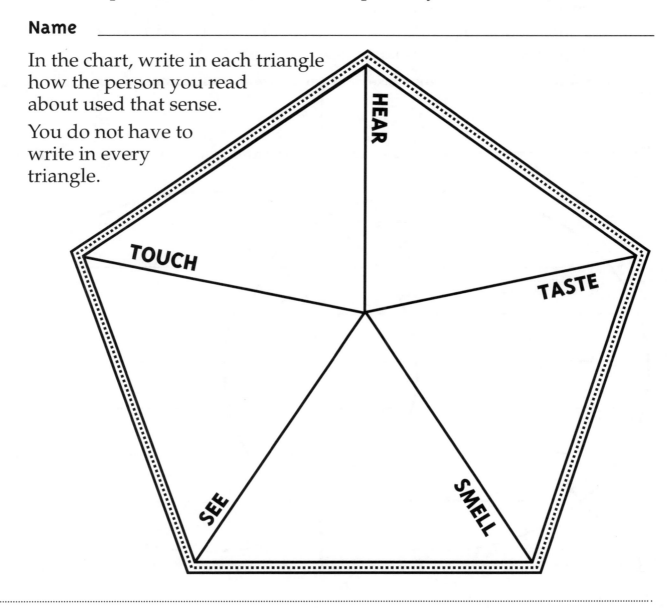

B. Did the Sense Chart help you to understand the person better? Why or why not? Write your answer on the back of this sheet.

Name _____ Date _____

Using a Venn Diagram

> A **Venn Diagram** can help you to **compare** and **contrast** two people. The part of the diagram where the circles overlap tells how the people are **alike**. The parts that do not overlap tell how the people are **different**.

A. Compare two people from the book. Use the Venn Diagram to show how the people are alike and different. To begin, write the names of the two people in the two boxes below.

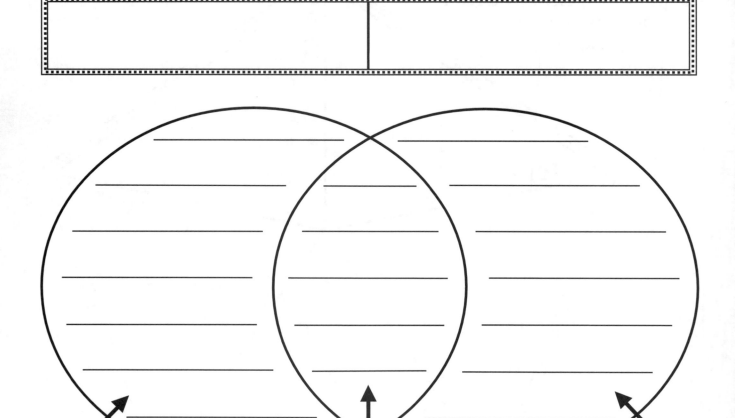

differences

similarities

differences

B. Read the question below. Then use the back of this sheet to answer it.

How can a Venn Diagram help you with your writing?

Name _____ Date _____

Using a K-W-L Chart

A **K-W-L Chart** helps you to organize your thoughts before, while, and after you read. Before you read, write what you **K**now about the person in the first column. In the second column, write what you **W**ant to learn about the person. After you read, write what you have **L**earned in the third column.

Write the name of the person you will read about. Then fill in the three columns of the chart. Fill in column **L** after you read the book.

Name _____

K	W	L

Biography

Name _____ Date _____

Using an Encyclopedia

An **encyclopedia** is arranged in alphabetical order. For example, the topic "Harriet Tubman" would appear in Volume 8 because TU comes after SAU and before USP. Names of people are listed last-name first.

An encyclopedia has **guide words** at the top of each page. They tell the first entry on the left-hand page and last entry on the right-hand page.

A. Read the questions below. Write your answers on the lines.

1. Suppose you want to learn more about the person you just read about. Which encyclopedia volume would you select? _____

2. Look on the back cover of the book you just read. Choose another famous person. Whom did you choose? _____ Which volume would have information about this person? _____

B. Look at the guide words below. Between which guide words would you find each topic? Fill in the letter that matches the guide words.

A. bear/bench	B. ear/folk tale	C. delegate/equal rights	D. forest/grapes

3. Frederick Douglass   Ⓐ   Ⓑ   Ⓒ   Ⓓ

4. Amelia Earhart   Ⓐ   Ⓑ   Ⓒ   Ⓓ

5. Benjamin Franklin   Ⓐ   Ⓑ   Ⓒ   Ⓓ

C. Choose one event in the life of the person you read about. Look it up in an encyclopedia. On the back of this sheet, write three new facts.

Name _____ Date _____

Using the Parts of a Book

> Knowing about the **parts of a book** can help you find information quickly.
> Here are some parts of the book you are reading.
>   **Title Page:** Tells the name of the book, the author, and the publisher
>   **Table of Contents:** Lists all the parts of the book in order
>   **Important Dates:** Lists important events in the person's life
>   **Words to Know:** Defines important words
>   **Read More:** Lists other books about the person
>   **Useful Addresses:** Lists places that have information about the person

A. Write your answers on the lines. Use the book to help you.

1. What is the title of the first chapter? _____

2. What is one place you can write to if you want more information about

   the person you read about? _____

   Write down the address of the place. _____

   _____

   _____

   Where did you find this information? _____

3. Which page tells about the person's childhood? _____

4. Look at the **Important Dates** section. Which event do you think is the

   most important? Why? _____

   _____

B. Compare the parts of this book to another book in your classroom.
Which parts of these books are the same? Which parts are different?
Write your answer on the back of this sheet.

Biography

Name _____ Date _____

Using the Internet

> You can use the **Internet** to help you research a topic. The **home page** of a site
> for your topic is the place to begin. It usually gives **links** to other pages. Click
> on the link that interests you to find more about your topic.

A. Log on to the Internet. Type in the following address:
http://www.biography.com

1. What is the title of the home page? _____

2. In the blank box on the home page, type the name of the person you
just read about. Double-click *Find*.

3. Now click on the name of the person read about. You will go to a new
screen. This screen will give you some information about the person.

4. Look at the information. Write three important facts you learn about
this person.

_____

_____

_____

B. Click on the following address: **http://www.greatwomen.org.** Choose a
woman. Write her name and something important that she did.

_____

_____

_____

_____

_____

Name _____ Date _____

Using an Almanac

An **almanac** is a book that gives facts about many topics. Some topics are news events, weather, nature, and geography. An almanac has many **charts** and **tables**, is published once a year, and has up-to-date information.

A. Use an almanac to answer the questions below.

1. The person you just read about lived through important historical times. Think of one historical event that you know occurred during the person's lifetime. Write it on the line.

_____

On which page in the almanac can you find information about the event? Look in the **Index**. On the line, write down the page number or numbers where the information can be found.

_____

2. Look for a list of all the U.S. Presidents. Who were the U.S. Presidents during the lifetime of the person you read about? _____

_____

B. Look in the **Important Dates** section of the book you just read.

- Choose three events that are listed. Write the dates in the first column of the chart below. Write the events in the second column.
- Look in the almanac for a time line of world events. Which events were happening at the same time? Write one event in the third column for each event in the second column.

DATE	EVENT IN BIOGRAPHY	WORLD EVENT

Name _____ Date _____

Using a Thesaurus

> A **thesaurus** can help you find words that have the same or almost the same meaning. These words are called **synonyms**. A thesaurus also can help you find words that have opposite meanings. These words are called **antonyms**.

A. Use the thesaurus in your classroom to answer these questions. Write your answers on the lines.

1. Look up the word *history* in the thesaurus. What are the word's

    synonyms? _____

2. Choose one of the synonyms you found. Write a sentence using the word. Your sentence should be about the person you just read about.

    _____

    _____

3. What synonyms are listed for *famous*? _____

4. What antonyms are listed for *famous*? _____

5. Which antonym do you think is the most opposite in meaning to

    famous? Write it here. _____

6. Write a sentence using the antonym you chose. _____

    _____

B. Reread one paragraph from your book. Choose three words from the paragraph. Find a synonym for each word. Rewrite the paragraph and replace the words with the synonyms you found. Use the back of this sheet for your answer.

Compare your new paragraph with the paragraph in the book. Which paragraph is better, and why? Use the back of this sheet to write your answer.

Figure 5.6 shows how the Land/Creighton farm may have looked during the 1860s. The picture is based upon the recollections of family members and the description given in the novel.

FIG. 5.6. Illustrated map of the Land/Creighton farm.

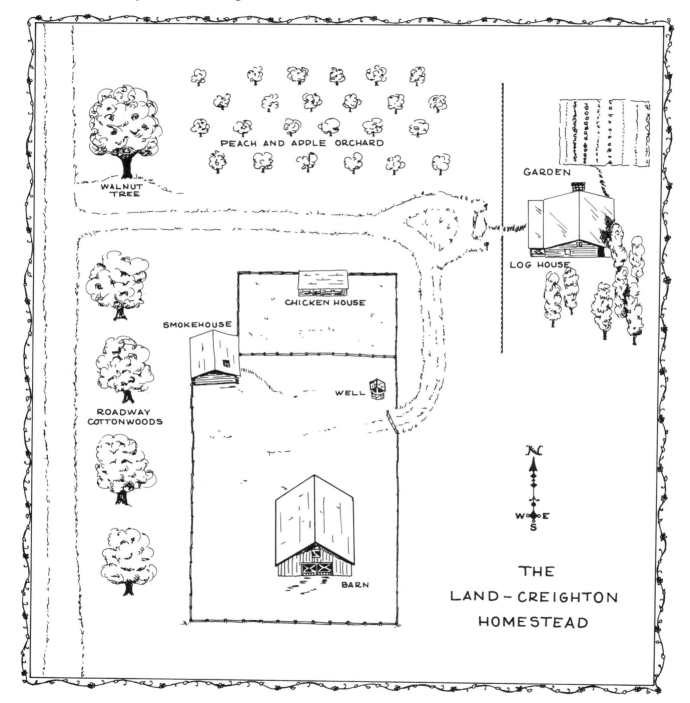

The trees in figure 5.7 border a cornfield east of the house and they are old enough to have been around at the time of the Civil War. Their location fits the one given in the novel as Eb's hiding place when he deserted the Union ranks in March 1863.

FIG. 5.7. A stand of old oak trees east of the farm.

Jasper County had a population of 8,364 in 1860 and, in that same year, Newton had a population of 300. All communications were carried on by means of Joe Litzelmann's hack express, which made one trip daily between Newton and Olney, a metropolis of 1,260 with a railroad and a telegraph. Figure 5.8 shows the area transportation routes.

Two towns mentioned frequently in *Across Five Aprils* are Hidalgo and Rose Hill. Both towns are shown on maps of the 1860s and both had post offices, but neither was actually incorporated as a town until 1878, after the railway went through the area. In their peak years, around the turn of the century, both towns had many businesses including doctors' offices, mills, and churches. It was to Hidalgo that Ed Turner's oldest son was sent in search of the doctor when Matt Creighton was stricken with a heart attack. County records verify that there were several physicians in Hidalgo and Rose Hill at the time.

There were few good roads in Jasper County in the early 1860s. Maps of the time show common or unpaved roads from Newton to Greenup in the north, to Palestine in the east, to Effingham in the west, to Olney in the south and to Louisville in the southwest. The towns of Newton, Rose Hill, and Hidalgo were connected by the road that ran north to Greenup. The road was blazed in 1836 during an era of transportation expansion in the county. In that same year a road to Effingham was projected, and by 1844 there were roads connecting Newton to Olney, Vandalia, and Marion County. The roads were crudely graded and none were easy to travel. There was no paved highway out of Newton until 1921.

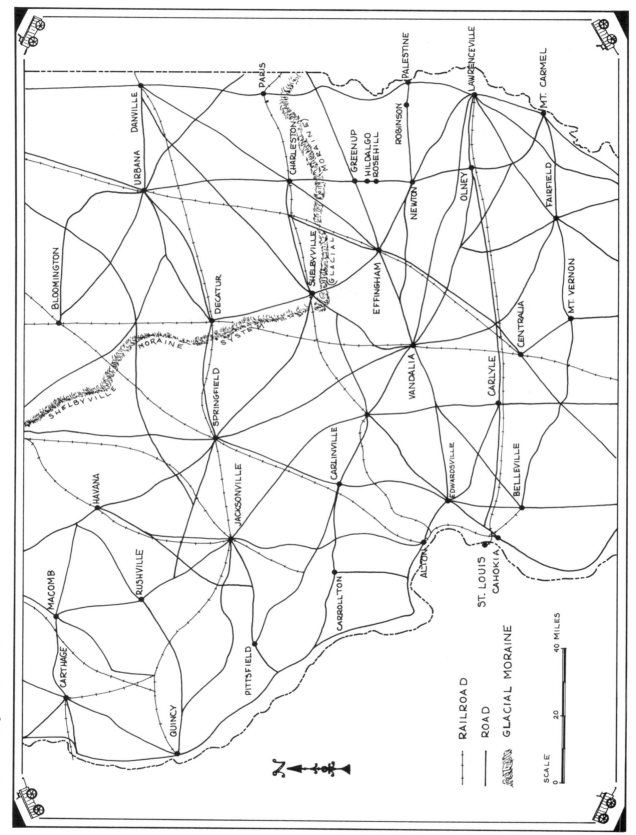

FIG. 5.8. Illinois Transportation Routes.

Figure 5.9 shows the early road that was used to travel north out of Newton. The 15 miles from the Land homestead to Newton took at least four hours by horse and buggy.

FIG. 5.9. The old road leading north out of Newton.

There was a bridge built across the Embarras River at Newton in 1857 at a cost of $4,350, but it collapsed and had to be rebuilt in 1861.

Jethro and his family would have crossed the bridge that stood at the site in figure 5.10 when they came to Newton. This present steel bridge was built in 1890, replacing the earlier wooden structure.

FIG. 5.10. The new, steel bridge at Newton that has replaced the original wooden bridge.

Irene Hunt describes Newton in 1861 as a rather dreary little village with a town square and jail, two feed stores, a harness shop, two general stores, a newspaper office, three saloons, and a restaurant. County records show that by 1874, the population of Newton had grown to 400 and there were eight stores, a newspaper, two saloons, two hotels, one courthouse, and one mill (see fig. 5.11). There was a postmaster, and the mail was carried in on horseback once a week.

Point Pleasant had grown, too. Now there were two blacksmith and wagon shops in addition to the general store. Eighteen or 20 people resided in the village at that time.

FIG. 5.11. The Newton town square.

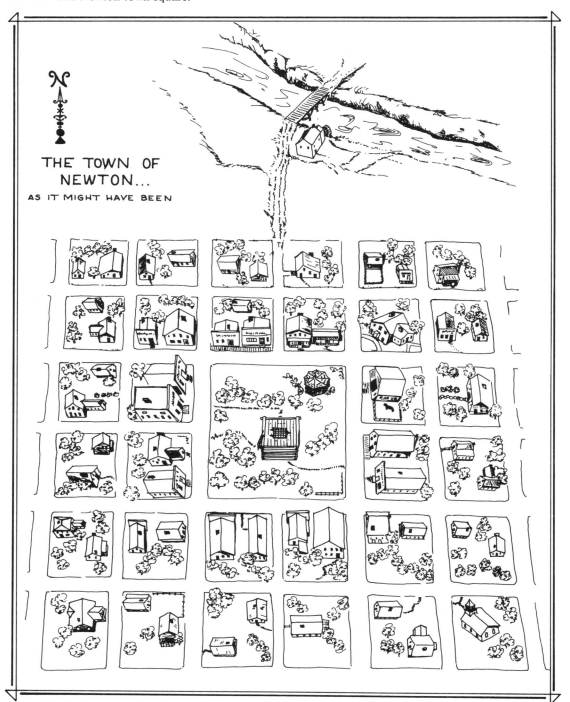

THE TOWN OF NEWTON...

AS IT MIGHT HAVE BEEN

Jasper County Today

In 1870, after the Civil War, the county population was 11,234 and 110 years later, in 1980, it had grown to only 11,318.

During the intervening years, however, the population had almost doubled, peaking at 20,160 in 1900.

Table 5.1.

Population Statistics

	1860	1880	1900	1920	1930	1980
Jasper County	8,364	14,515	20,160	16,064	12,809	11,318
Newton	300	1,168	1,630	2,083	2,076	3,186
Hidalgo		35	190	193	153	161
Rose Hill		199	229	202	179	121

The table above illustrates the shift in population over the years. Small towns have declined, but Newton, the county seat and trading center for farmers in the Embarras River valley, has grown to 3,186. Many villages, such as Point Pleasant, have disappeared completely. A similar decline has occurred in the number of small farms of up to 100 acres in the county, while the number of large farms of 1,000 acres or more has increased somewhat.

Figure 5.12 shows all that remains of Point Pleasant. To the far right is the site of the Land farm. When originally settled in the 1830s, about one-third of the area was timbered, in fact the first business in Newton was a sawmill. The old mill on the Embarras River (fig. 5.13) has been renovated and today houses a restaurant.

FIG. 5.12. The sign marks where Point Pleasant once stood.

FIG. 5.13. The Newton Sawmill.

In the 1860s there was an abundant and varied wildlife population. Today there are still forested areas, and several species of wild animals remain. The Jasper County Prairie Chicken Reserve is a 77-acre sanctuary that supports the majority of the 300 to 400 endangered birds of that species that remain in Illinois. Other natural areas include the Sam Parr State Park (fig. 5.14), which is less than 8 miles south of the Land homestead. In the park are hiking trails, camping facilities, and a 180-acre lake that is well stocked with fish.

FIG. 5.14. This area of the Sam Parr State Park is reminiscent of the landscape seen by early settlers in Jasper County.

Newton Lake Fish and Wildlife Area in the southwestern section of the county opened to the public in 1980. It has 1,755 acres, and the activities offered are fishing, boating, hiking, skiing, and horseback riding. Peterson Park, in Newton, is made up of 28 acres on the south side of the Embarras River.

Sandstone and limestone rock lie under the soil of the county, and some deposits of coal are found although no coal is currently being mined. Oil wells have operated around the countryside for years, and today the county is dotted with producing wells.

The glacier, to which Jethro refers in chapter 1, stopped less than 30 miles north of Newton, contributing to the formation of the rich soil in the area. A section of the moraine south of Charleston, Illinois, is shown in figure 5.15.

FIG. 5.15. A country road south of Charleston rolls over the moraine.

The fictional editor of the county paper was a friend of the Creighton family in Irene Hunt's novel, and Jasper County has had many newspapers over the years; there were two in publication during the Civil War. Today the Newton Press Mentor has its office on the west side of the square.

Although the county is primarily agricultural, there are several industries that contribute to the economy of the area. A broom factory is in operation in Newton, along with a clothing manufacturer and an automotive products company.

The well-stocked Newton Public Library is conveniently located on the town square. Its holdings include a small local history collection, and in the back of the library is a historical museum that especially features items from the Civil War era. Newton is pictured in figure 5.16.

FIG. 5.16. Newton is a quiet, friendly little town.

FOR MORE INFORMATION

Jasper County Historical and Genealogical Society, Inc.
c/o Newton Public Library
100 South Van Buren St.
Newton, IL 62448

NOTE

[1]Glenn W. Sutherland, ed., *New and Complete History of Jasper County and the 1884 History of Jasper County* (Evansville, IN: Unigraphic, 1974), 145-48.

EXTENDED ACTIVITIES

1. Using the map of Jasper County (map A — Hunt):

   a. Plot Jethro's probable route from his home to Newton.

   b. If his horse and wagon traveled at 4 miles per hour, how long would it take him to get to Newton?

   c. Write a brief description of what the journey would be like today in modern vehicles and on current roads. How long would the trip take now?

2. Compare the speed with which news of the war arrived at the Creighton farm to the speed with which we learned of the events taking place in Operation Desert Storm during January 1991. How do you account for the time differences?

3. On the Civil War battlefield map (map B — Hunt), mark those battles in which, as recounted in the story, the Creighton boys and their friends participated. Indicate which character was in a particular battle by circling the location in the following colors:

   Eb — green
   Tom — red
   John — black
   Shad — yellow
   Bill — blue

4. The year is 1860. You are a settler who has recently arrived in Jasper County and you are looking for land to buy. You want to build a home and begin farming. Consult the 1860 county map and select a good spot for your farm. Do the following:

   a. Explain why you decided to buy property in that location.

   b. Now that you have selected a site for your farm, draw a plan so that construction can begin. This plan should be like a map; it must be drawn to scale and must have a key. Include the cabin, well, garden, barn, fields, pastures, orchards, and smokehouse, as well as anything else you think is necessary. Take into consideration any natural land features such as creeks, forests, and hills.

5. In the first chapter of the story Jethro regrets the fact that the last glacier melted before it got to his region of Illinois, allowing the formation of dark, rich soil far to the north. On map C — Hunt trace the location of the moraine (where the glacier stopped). What discrepancy do you find between its location on the map and the information Jethro gives the reader about where the glacier melted?

6. Using map B — Hunt and map C — Brink in chapter three, plot the probable route to Washington taken by Jenny and Ross Milton.

Map A—Hunt

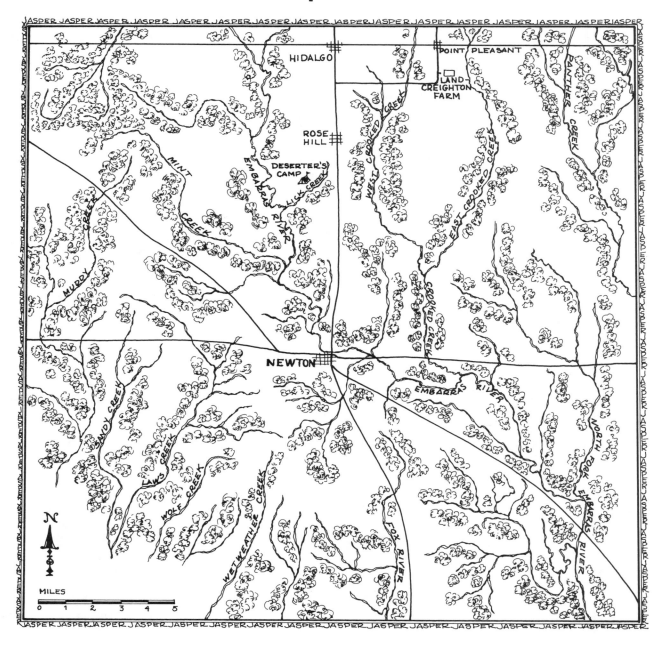

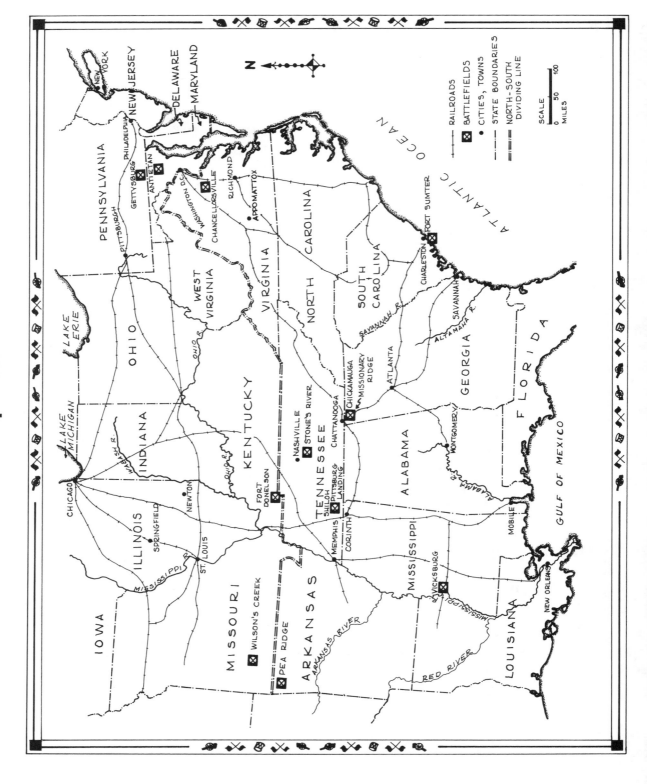

Map B—Hunt

Map C—Hunt

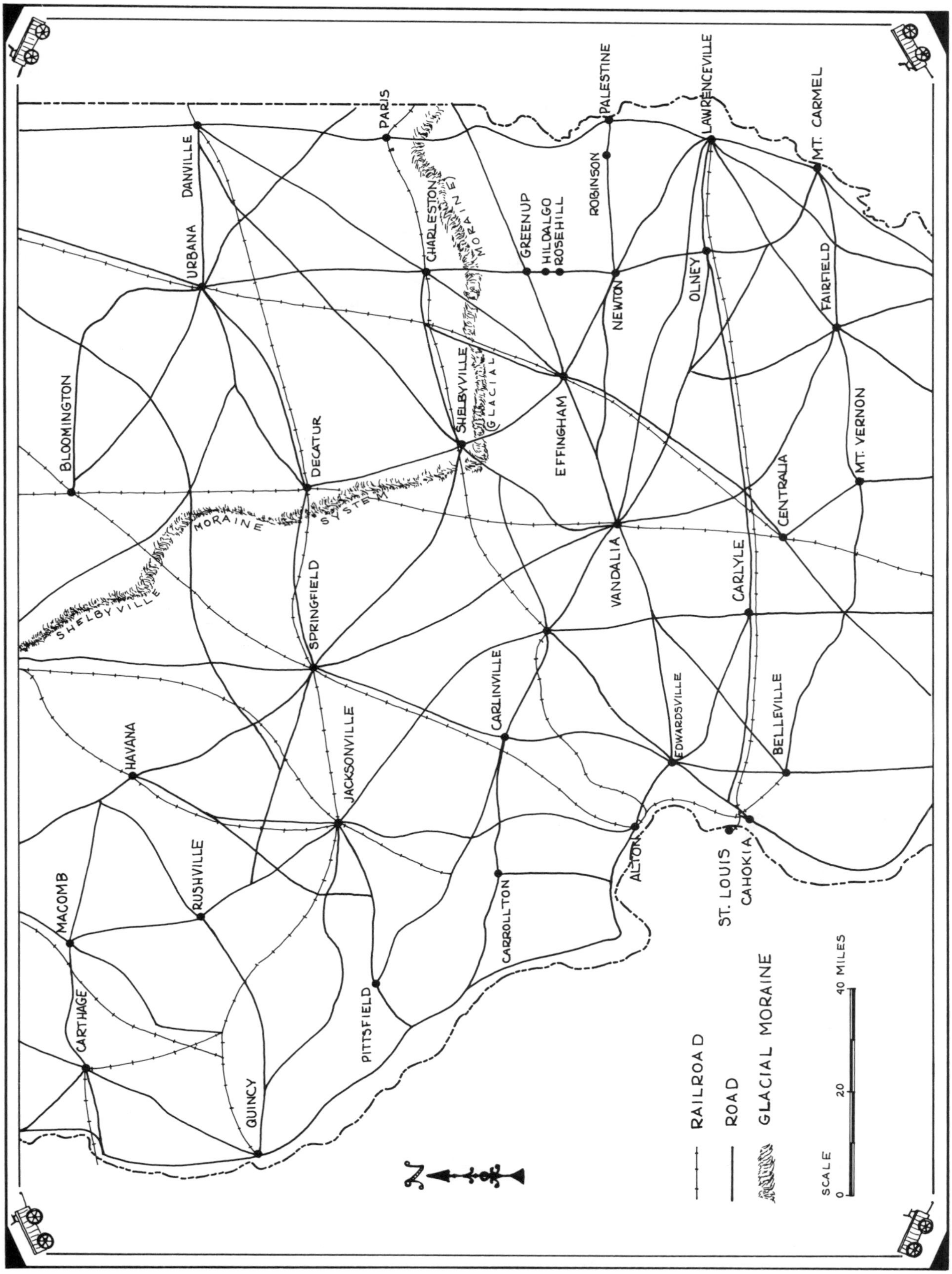

From *On Location*, 1992. Teacher Ideas Press, a Division of Libraries Unlimited, P.O. Box 6633, Englewood, CO 80155-6633

QUESTIONS FOR DISCUSSION

1. What factors led to the population growth of Newton over the hundred years between 1880 and 1980, as opposed to the disappearance of Point Pleasant and the lack of growth of the towns of Hidalgo and Rose Hill?

2. What factors will affect the continued existence of small, midwestern towns like Newton? What steps might be taken to insure their continued growth?

3. Today we have a variety of media sources to keep a wide cross section of the public informed about the news. Had these sources been available in 1861, what are some of the positive outcomes that might have been expected of a well-informed public? Could there have been any negative outcomes?

From *On Location*, 1992. Teacher Ideas Press, a Division of Libraries Unlimited, P.O. Box 6633, Englewood, CO 80155-6633

SUGGESTED READING

Other Books by Irene Hunt

The Everlasting Hills. New York: Scribner, 1985. 184 pages.

Jeremy is a slightly retarded 12-year-old living with his father and older sister in the mountains of Colorado. He is emotionally abused by his bitter, uncaring father, so he runs away and is taken in by Ishmael, a kindly old man who lives alone. Ishmael helps Jeremy to gain confidence in himself and acts as a bridge between the estranged father and son.

Lottery Rose: A Novel. New York: Scribner, 1976. 185 pages.

This is a story of the physical abuse of 7-year-old Georgie who suffers at the hands of his mother's boyfriend. He is rescued at last by the police, and his recovery from his psychic and physical wounds seems assured.

No Promises in the Wind. Chicago: Follett, 1970. 247 pages.

The time is 1932, the Great Depression. Josh is only 15 but he is bitterly aware of the desperate struggle to survive in the world around him and even more aware of the struggles within himself.

Trail of Apple Blossoms. Chicago: Follett, 1968. 64 pages.

This brief story of John Chapman focuses on his philosophy and his personality as it tells of his relationship with wild creatures and humans, his courage and his love of peace.

Up a Road Slowly. Chicago: Follett, 1966. 192 pages.

Julie Trelling is only 7 years old when her mother dies and she is sent to live with her strict Aunt Cordelia. Over the next 10 years Julie deals with the problems of jealousy, strained family relationships, an alcoholic uncle, the death of a friend, and a first love. She has grown in wisdom and maturity by the time her college days are near. Winner of the 1967 Newbery Medal.

William. New York: Scribner, 1977. 188 pages.

A family of three black children struggles to stay together when their mother dies leaving them alone. Cared for by a young, white, unwed mother, they manage to survive as a family for three years before internal strife and outside pressures threaten to break up their household.

The United States Civil War

Catton, Bruce. *This Hallowed Ground; The Story of the Union Side of the Civil War*. New York: Doubleday, 1956. 437 pages.

The entire scope of the war is dealt with here from the restless months before the conflict to the Confederate surrender.

Gauch, Patricia Lee. *Thunder at Gettysburg*. New York: Coward, McCann & Geoghegan, 1975. 46 pages.

For three days Tillie Pierce lived with the reality of war when she was separated from her family on the battlefield at Gettysburg.

Hicken, Victor. *Illinois in the Civil War*. Urbana, Illinois: University of Illinois Press, 1966. 391 pages.
  Nearly 35,000 young men from Illinois lost their lives in the Civil War, but thousands of others left their Illinois hometowns in 1861 and returned in 1865. The role of common soldiers is related here through actual quotes from diaries and letters.

Jordan, Robert Paul. *The Civil War*. Washington, D.C.: National Geographic, 1969. 215 pages.
  Drawings, photographs, and paintings enhance this survey of the battles and leaders in the war.

Levenson, Dorothy. *The First Book of the Civil War*. New York: Watts, 1977. 66 pages.
  The life of the soldier, the position of women, slavery, and taxes are among the issues discussed.

Murphy, Jim. *The Boys' War: Confederate and Union Soldiers Talk about the Civil War*. New York: Clarion, 1990. 110 pages.
  Based on first-hand accounts and illustrated with archival photographs, this book gives a vivid picture of the Civil War and the young boys who fought in it.

Ray, Delia. *A Nation Torn: The Story of How the Civil War Began*. New York: Lodestar, 1990. 102 pages.
  The events leading up to the war are vividly detailed.

Werstein, Irving. *The Many Faces of the Civil War*. New York: Messner, 1961. 192 pages.
  The emphasis here is on the personalities and deeds of the leading figures of the war.

The United States Civil War (Fiction)

Beatty, Patricia. *Charley Skedaddle*. New York: Morrow, 1987. 186 pages.
  City slicker Charlie Quinn, a cocky Bowery Boy, runs away and joins the Union army. He bolts during his first encounter with the horrors of war and takes refuge in the mountains of Virginia.

Beatty, Patricia. *Turn Homeward, Hanalee*. New York: Morrow, 1984. 193 pages.
  Hanalee and her brother Jem are taken from their Georgia home and shipped to Indiana where they are offered as workers to anyone who wants them. The story is based upon an actual Civil War incident.

Lunn, Janet. *The Root Cellar*. New York: Scribner, 1983. 229 pages.
  When she is orphaned, Rose is sent to live in a new home where she feels she does not belong. When she takes refuge in the root cellar she finds she has traveled back in time to Civil War days where she befriends the war-torn residents of the house.

Abraham Lincoln

Freedman, Russell. *Lincoln: A Photobiography*. New York: Clarion Books, 1987. 149 pages.
  The winner of the 1988 Newbery Medal, this detailed history of Lincoln's life is enlivened by dozens of photographs and drawings.

Miers, Earl Schenk. *Abraham Lincoln in Peace and War*. New York: American Heritage, 1964. 153 pages.
  A taste of the times is given in this work, which is lavishly documented with photographs, maps, newspaper clippings, and paintings.

North, Sterling. *Abe Lincoln: Log Cabin to White House*. New York: Random House, 1987 (originally published in 1956). 150 pages.
The emphasis here is on Lincoln's humble beginnings and early career.

Life in the 1860s

Cross, Helen Reeder. *Life in Lincoln's America*. New York: Random House, 1964. 171 pages.
Information is given in interesting text, photographs, and drawings about work and play, trade and travel, from 1800 to 1860.

Foster, Genevieve. *Abraham Lincoln's World*. New York: Scribner, 1944. 347 pages.
Learn what was happening all over the world during Lincoln's lifetime.

————. *Year of Lincoln*. New York: Scribner, 1970. 64 pages.
This book explains the significance of central figures of world importance during the early Civil War period.

Sandler, Martin W. *The Way We Lived: A Photographic Record of Work in a Vanished America*. Boston: Little, Brown, 1977. 120 pages.
Old photographs portray what it was like to work for a living between 1865 and 1900.

American Newspapers

Fisher, Leonard Everett. *The Newspapers*. New York: Holiday House, 1981. 62 pages.
The growth of the newspaper industry is traced from the beginning of the 1800s to the present. Of special interest is the information on the press coverage of the Civil War.

LITTLE HOUSE IN THE BIG WOODS ANSWER KEY

1. The Big Woods supplied wood for cooking and heating fuel. It supplied meat, berries, nuts, honey, and other food for the Ingalls family. They got some of their clothing from the skins of animals and furniture from the timber. Their house was made from logs, and stones from the creek banks were used in the construction of the chimney. Water came from a well. Today food is usually purchased in supermarkets, fuel comes from underground pipes or is delivered in large tanks. Homes are constructed from materials often shipped long distances. Our clothing is almost always purchased from stores.

2. Pictures should show the growth of the town, new roads, and the increase in farmland in ratio to the woodland.

3. Consult figure 1.14 for accuracy.

4. Answers will vary.

5. Answers will vary but should include access to transportation and shipping routes, fresh water, plentiful game, timber for shelter and fuel.

6. Chicago, Illinois = 395 miles northwest
    Duluth, Minnesota, and Superior, Wisconsin = 170 miles south
    Eau Claire, Wisconsin = 40 miles southwest
    Green Bay, Wisconsin = 210 miles west
    La Crosse, Wisconsin = 65 miles northwest
    Madison, Wisconsin = 170 miles northwest
    Milwaukee, Wisconsin = 240 miles northwest
    Minneapolis — St. Paul, Minnesota = 60 miles southeast
    Oshkosh, Wisconsin = 185 miles northwest
    Wausau, Wisconsin = 130 miles southwest

7. Lake Pepin is actually a wide place in the Mississippi River.

8. This part of Wisconsin is marked by rolling hills and ridges. The area is partly wooded with mixed evergreen and deciduous forests. Several small streams cut through the countryside. Today the economy is primarily agricultural, with many dairy and livestock farms. The state of Wisconsin is first in the nation in the production of milk, cheese, butter, and sweetened condensed milk. The climate is marked by long, severe winters and short, warm summers. The average temperature is 43°F, but extremes of 114°F and -34°F have been recorded. The average annual rainfall is 31 inches and the average snowfall is 45 inches.

9. Sailing, waterskiing, fishing, snowmobiling, cross-country skiing, hiking, swimming, ice boating, skating, canoeing, and hunting are enjoyed around Pepin today. In Laura's day waterskiing, snowmobiling, and ice boating would have been unknown.

10 through 13. Answers will vary.

ON MY HONOR ANSWER KEY

1. a. Vermilion River
   Illinois River
   Mississippi River

   b. Illinois
   Missouri
   Kentucky
   Tennessee
   Arkansas
   Mississippi
   Louisiana

2. Vermilion River
   LaSalle County
   Livingston County

   Little Vermilion River
   LaSalle County

   Vermilion River (South)
   Vermilion County, Illinois
   Vermilion County, Indiana

3. Forms of transportation shown include:
   Riverboats on the Illinois River
   Interstate highways I-80 and I-39
   Railroads: Burlington Northern and Illinois Central

4. Answers will vary.

5. City parks:
    Lehigh Memorial Park
    Memorial Park
    City Park

    State parks:
    Starved Rock State Park
    Matthiessen State Park

6. Answers will vary.

7. a. It is about 6 miles to the park via State Route 71 to Jonesville.

    b. It is about 4.5 miles from the city hall to the visitor's center at Starved Rock via Ed Hand Road.

    c. Joel's father's estimate was the most correct.

8. a. $F = 8$

    b. $F = 3$

    c. $C = 2$

    d. $E = 4$

9. He descended about 100 feet.

    While pushing his bike, he would have climbed about 100 feet.

10. a. Ordovician

    b. Stone, silica sand, portland cement, building stone, crude oil, gas, zinc, lead

    c. The largest industry is a cement factory, and the natural resources of the area include the materials necessary for the production of cement.

    d. The economy and industry in an area are in part determined by the available natural resources.

CADDIE WOODLAWN AND *MAGICAL MELONS* ANSWER KEY

1. a. CC north to SS.
        SS northeast to N.
        N north to U.S. Route 10.
        U.S. Route 10 southeast to State Route 25.
        State Route 25 north to Caddie Woodlawn home and park.

    b. About 22 miles

    c. Dunn County

    d. Pepin County; Durand is the county seat.

2. a. 1. A-5
        2. B-6
        3. D-1
        4. C-6

    b. Check answers for accuracy.

    c. About 3.5 miles

3. No. Laura Ingalls was born in 1867, the year the Woodhouses left Dunnville.

4. The town has nearly vanished. Only a few houses remain. The steamer no longer makes the trip up the Menomonie River. There is no lumbering industry to support the local economy. The railroad bypassed the town and the county seat was moved from Dunnville to Menomonie.

5. Uncle Edmund took Nero to St. Louis.

    a. Check answers for accuracy.

    b. 615 miles

6. Answers will vary.

7. Answers will vary.

8. Answers will vary.

9. Most of the news arrived by mail when the steamboat made the trip to Dunnville. Sometimes news was relayed by travelers who stopped at the farm. Today we receive national and world news through television, radio, newspapers, magazines, and even computerized electronic sources.

10. Earth
    Western Hemisphere
    North American Continent
    United States of America
    North Central Region
    Wisconsin
    Dunn County
    Downsville
    State Highway 25

11. The part of Wisconsin where Caddie lived is marked by rolling hills and ridges. The area is partly wooded with mixed evergreen and deciduous forests. Several small streams cut through the countryside.

    Today the economy is primarily agricultural, with many dairy and livestock farms. The state of Wisconsin is first in the nation in the production of milk, cheese, butter, and sweetened condensed milk. The climate is marked by long, severe winters and short, warm summers. The average temperature is 43°F, but extremes of 114°F and -34°F have been recorded. The average annual rainfall is 31 inches, and the average snowfall is 45 inches.

12. a. Caddie's home = 160 acres
 Laura's home = 40 acres

 b. Caddie's home = sawn boards
 Laura's home = logs

 c. 1. Caddie's home = 2,067 square feet
 Laura's home = 546 square feet

 2. Caddie's home = 8 rooms, including attic
 Laura's home = 4 rooms, including loft

 3. Caddie's home = 18 windows
 Laura's home = 3 windows

 4. Caddie's home = 2 fireplaces
 Laura's home = 1 fireplace

13. Answers will vary, but the items to consider include:

 a. Distance to town
 Caddie = about ¾ mile
 Laura = 7 miles

 b. Father's occupation
 Caddie's father = millwright
 Laura's father = hunter and farmer

 c. Number in household
 Caddie = 8 family members, plus at least 2 employees
 Laura's family = 5 family members

 d. Previous home
 Caddie = Boston
 Laura = eastern Wisconsin

RASCAL ANSWER KEY

1. a. 3
 b. 4
 c. 1
 d. 6
 e. 2
 f. 5

2. a. 6
 b. 2
 c. 3
 d. 4
 e. 5
 f. 1

3. a. Using the route given in the book, Albion Street north and across Saunders Creek, it would have been 1.5 miles. If a present-day route were taken (West Rollin and north on Stoughton past the Conservation Park), it would be 1.75 miles.

    b. 2.5 miles

    c. About 10 miles

    d. Rock County

    e. Jefferson County

    f. Southwest

    g. Northeast

4. The Brule River that Sterling and his father visited is about 35 miles east of Superior, Wisconsin. The other Brule forms part of the Michigan/Wisconsin boundary in northeastern Wisconsin. The probable route might have been as follows:

Wisconsin Route 106 to Ft. Atkinson, then

Wisconsin 26 to U.S. 151, then

U.S. 41 from Fon du Lac to Green Bay, then on to Ashland (some creativity and imagination may be employed when tracing the route from Green Bay to Ashland, as there are no reference points given in the text), and finally

Wisconsin 2 from Ashland to the Brule River.

5. a. The Mississippi River/Lake Michigan watershed line is marked on the map. It runs from north to south through the middle of the state to Portage, then east to Milwaukee and south to Chicago.

    b. Saunders Creek
Rock River
Mississippi River
Gulf of Mexico

    c. Capable students with access to detailed maps may be expected to include the starred items below:
      Lake Winnebago
      Fox River
      Green Bay
      Lake Michigan
      *Straits of Mackinac
      Lake Huron
      *St. Clair River
      *Lake St. Clair
      *Detroit River
      Lake Erie
      *Niagara River
      Lake Ontario
      St. Lawrence River
      Atlantic Ocean

    d.   Brule River
           Lake Superior
         *Whitefish Bay
         *Lake George to St. Joseph Channel to North Channel or an alternative route might be from
           Lake Nicolet to Munuscong Lake to Poyagannissing Bay
           Lake Huron
         *St. Clair River
         *Lake St. Clair
         *Detroit River
           Lake Erie
         *Niagara River
           Lake Ontario
           St. Lawrence River
           Atlantic Ocean

    e.   Yes. C and D would meet in northern Lake Huron.

6.   Answers will vary.

7.   Edgerton 42.49 N 89.06 W

8.   The climate of Wisconsin is marked by short, hot summers and long, cold winters. The average yearly temperature is 43°F, and the average annual rainfall is 30 to 35 inches. The average annual snowfall is 45 inches. Edgerton is located in Wisconsin's central plain, typified by flat expanses and low, rounded hills cut by small streams and lakes. The natural vegetation in the area is deciduous trees and grasses.

9.   Interstate 90 passes 2 miles from Edgerton, and U.S. Route 51 and State Route 59 bisect the town. The Rock County airport is located just 15 miles away, south of Janesville, and the Madison airport is 30 miles north. There is a private airport 3 miles north of Edgerton that is open to the public. The Chicago, Milwaukee, St. Paul and Pacific Railroad still runs through town. The economy of Edgerton is based on agriculture, especially the growing and harvesting of tobacco. The population density for the area around Edgerton is 25-60 per square mile.

10.   Answers will vary.

11.   Answers will vary.

ACROSS FIVE APRILS ANSWER KEY

1. Several routes are possible, but the shortest is about 15 miles long. It would have taken Jethro about three and one-half or four hours to travel to Newton. Have students use a current road atlas to identify Illinois Route 130. The trip today takes about 20 minutes.

2. Instant information was available to the American public during Operation Desert Storm, thanks to satellite transmission of television signals at the speed of light, which takes only seconds to travel the 22,000 miles to the satellite and back. In the 1860s, rural families in southern Illinois awaited war news carried in newspapers, which were delivered by train and horseback. St. Louis newspapers were sent to Olney on the railroad, then to Newton by horse and buggy. Details were often scarce because most news was transmitted by telegraph. For example, the Battle of Shiloh took place on April 6 and 7, 1862, and the Creightons first learned of it during the second week in April. The details of the battle, however, drifted in over the course of a month in letters from soldiers at the front and by word of mouth. It wasn't until well after their barn had been burned on May 10th that they learned of Tom's death in that battle.

3. Eb (green)
    Donalson
    Pittsburg Landing (Shiloh)
    Vicksburg
   Tom (red)
    Donalson
    Pittsburg Landing (Shiloh)
   John (black)
    Stones River
    Chickamauga
    Missionary Ridge
    Nashville
   Shad (yellow)
    Antietam
    Fredericksburg
    Chancellorsville
    Gettysburg
   Bill (blue)
    Nashville

4. a. Answers will vary but consideration should be given to access to roads, forests, water, drainage, and the distance to centers of population.

   b. Have students display their maps and explain any unique features.

5. The Shelbyville Morainic System is only about 35 miles north of Newton. Jethro said the glacier melted about 100 miles to the north.

6. The route as described in the book is from Olney to St. Louis and then on to Washington by railway.

ACROSS FIVE APRILS—POSSIBILITIES FOR DISCUSSION

1. When the primary means of transportation was on foot or horse, it was important to have stores, schools, churches, medical care and other necessities relatively close at hand. With the advent of the automobile and improved roads it became possible to have access to necessary services quickly and in relative comfort despite weather conditions. Larger trading centers offered a broader selection of goods and services and thus attracted farmers who previously supported the small town economy.

   School districts found that bussing made consolidation of one-room schools possible. For some communities, like those in Jasper County, this made good sense economically and educationally because more academic and extracurricular opportunities could be offered for less cost to a larger number of students.

   Agricultural mechanization led to the growth of large farming operations and the decline of the small, family farm. With the help of farm machinery it became possible for one family to work larger blocks of land, and fewer families were needed to make the land productive, so the population in the rural areas declined.

2. If farms continue to grow in size, resulting in the further reduction of the rural population, communities such as Newton will shrink and possibly disappear. If the railroads discontinue service, there would be a negative impact on small towns. The growth of large shopping malls in cities within a reasonable driving distance will lure local shoppers to those distant markets, and local businesses will suffer.

   Encourage students to think broadly and creatively in developing solutions to the problems of rural America. High technology offers opportunities for employees to work in their homes, often in areas distant from their offices. Through electronic data transmission, workers can be productive even when far from the workplace. Quiet and friendly small towns may offer the atmosphere desired by these hi-tech workers of the future, especially if existing natural recreational features are enhanced and the cultural and social aspects of the community are developed.

3. Answers will vary.

Index

About the Author

Joanne Kelly has had an active and avid interest in children's literature since she haunted Chicago's school and public libraries during her childhood. Her previous books, *The Battle of Books* and *Rebuses for Readers* (in collaboration with Pat Martin and Kay V. Grabow), have drawn upon her depth of knowledge about good plots, settings, and characters in books for young people, but she has long had an interest in the real places where stories happen. She has a B.S. in elementary education, an M.S. in library science, and a certificate of advanced study in library science, all from the University of Illinois. She has served as an elementary librarian for 24 years and as coordinator of the district libraries of the Urbana School District, Urbana, Illinois, for 9 years. She and her husband Chuck live in Champaign, Illinois. When Chuck is not taking pictures for Joanne's books, he is occupied as head of Engineering, Office of Instructional Resources, University of Illinois at Urbana-Champaign.

About the Illustrator

Pat Martin has earned bachelor's and master's degrees from the University of Illinois at Urbana-Champaign and is employed as an art coordinator at Publication Services in Champaign. Previously, during the time that her two children attended Thomas Paine Elementary School in Urbana, Pat volunteered in the library where Joanne Kelly was the librarian. Pat's work at the library provided her with an excellent outlet for her interest in children's literature and art. When her children went on to junior high school, Pat taught undergraduate mathematics at the University of Illinois at Urbana-Champaign, where she served for 7 years. At the same time that Pat began training for a career in graphic arts, Joanne Kelly began writing teacher resource books, which she asked Pat to illustrate. *On Location* is the third book on which they have collaborated.